messy endings and confusing conversations

Finn Lyric

Published by Finn Lyric, 2024.

While every precaution has been taken in the preparation of this book, the publisher assumes no responsibility for errors or omissions, or for damages resulting from the use of the information contained herein.

MESSY ENDINGS AND CONFUSING CONVERSATIONS

First edition. December 22, 2024.

Copyright © 2024 Finn Lyric.

ISBN: 979-8230084167

Written by Finn Lyric.

Blindsided

3

FINN LYRIC

No, I didn't see it coming
As I sat at your kitchen table.
Out of the blue it hit me.
"We can still be friends."
I was happy. You were not.
Where did I go wrong?
How could I be so wrong?
"We can still be friends."
It stings like a knife.
It paralyzes my body.
I can't find the words.
My mind is a cyclone.
"Just say something."
I can't.
How do I instantly orchestrate
The way to express the punch,
The words that don't hurt you,
The words that express pain?
"Just say something."
Can't you see the lump in my throat?
Can't you hear me gasping for air?
Can't you feel my heart breaking?

MESSY ENDINGS AND CONFUSING CONVERSATIONS

The first time you let go, it hurts.
You cling to it with bruised hands,
Gasping for breath as your nails break.
The second time you let go, it is scary.
You release as soon as your fingers ache.
You catch your breath as you watch it slip away.
The third time you are at peace.
You drop your grip at the first resistance.
You stare at the floor and know it is gone.
Now you have forgotten how to hold on to anything.
You no longer reach for things you loved.
Your broken hands can't hold on to anything.
Learn to hold again.
Oh dear God,
Learn to hold on again.

FINN LYRIC

You wearing old pajamas was enough.
I loved enough.
Falling asleep on the couch with you was enough.
I loved enough.
Brushing against you in the kitchen was enough.
I loved enough.
Sharing a cup of coffee in the morning was enough.
I loved enough.
A long hug before the flight was enough.
I loved enough.
The drive to the grocery store with you was enough.
I loved enough.
You were enough... I loved enough.

MESSY ENDINGS AND CONFUSING CONVERSATIONS

I would give up my success
To hold you one more time.
I would give up my breath
To dance by your side.
I would give up my sight
To hear that you love me one last time.

FINN LYRIC

I need to catch a long red light,
To let my chest rest on the steering wheel,
To catch my breath and wipe my eyes,
To let myself mourn what was us.
I can't keep driving and feel my heart.
The wheels keep turning.
A life doesn't just stop moving.
Heartbreak is a storm to drive through,
White knuckles clinching the wheel,
Rearview reminding me of where you've been.
The windshield is full of cracks.
I drive
All night
Waiting for a red light.

MESSY ENDINGS AND CONFUSING CONVERSATIONS

My heart thumps in code,
Trying to decipher
Your cryptic lips.
My heart decodes with hope.
My mind unwraps with doubts.
My skeptical brain protects
My wounded heart
While my ears play spectator
To your enigmatic voice.

FINN LYRIC

How can I find solitude
When I hear your voice in my mind?
How can I sleep
When I dream of your touch?
How can I eat
When you left me empty?

MESSY ENDINGS AND CONFUSING CONVERSATIONS

I will never be the phoenix.
I will never rise from ashes.
I am the mountain,
Built through millennia of
Friction,
Collision,
Pain,
Conflict,
Grit.
And I remain for all to see.

FINN LYRIC

"You are so disciplined, going to the gym so early."
It is because I have been staring at the ceiling all night
"You look like you've lost so much weight."
It is because I only eat once every two days.
"You are so focused and getting so much done."
It is because I must stay busy to keep her off my mind.

MESSY ENDINGS AND CONFUSING CONVERSATIONS

I smile
To stop the tears from falling.
I laugh
To stop the choke in my throat.
I straighten my back
To hide the pain in my stomach.
I stay silent
To keep my voice from cracking.
Just fake it through the moment

FINN LYRIC

My world is crashing around me.
The sky is splitting like my heart.
The lump in my throat is choking me.
I feel every bit of pain and despair.
You will never see it by the way I sit silently,
The way I clutch my hands under the table.
My stomach is a stone throbbing in my gut.
I push down the tears and steady my voice.
I cannot let you know the damage you've done.
I cannot let you feel an ounce of my pain.
The problem is I still love you
And I am emotionally superficial.

MESSY ENDINGS AND CONFUSING CONVERSATIONS

I have to stay away:
Not because I hate you
But because I can't stop
Loving you.
When I don't see you.
I can convince myself
We are done.
But when I see you.
I know you were my one.

FINN LYRIC

Just know I will be here,
Waiting for you to return.
But my heart will go on.
One day, someone will
Sweep me off my feet.
You will lose me forever.
Please
don't let that happen.

MESSY ENDINGS AND CONFUSING CONVERSATIONS

Damn, I am going to miss you.
Dinner tonight — our first as ex-lovers.
I watch as you command the room
And all I can think is, "I will miss her."
You are so kind and tell great jokes.
Everyone loves and admires you.
You smile and laugh. I watch you dance.
All I can think is, "I, alone, truly know you."
I know your fears and insecurities.
I know your grit and I know your fight.
I miss our time and all that you are.
Please tell me how I can make this right.

FINN LYRIC

I never want to taste the bitter pill of settling.
There is a high from chasing the impossible.
I do not have to grasp it or hold on.
Just to touch it with my fingertip.
The chase, the journey, or the pursuit.
I fully acknowledge this breaks my own heart.
I fully acknowledge that this gives me life.

Blindsided

MESSY ENDINGS AND CONFUSING CONVERSATIONS

I have to stay away:
Not because I hate you
But because I can't stop
Loving you.
When I don't see you.
I can convince myself
We are done.
But when I see you.
I know you were my one.

FINN LYRIC

Just know I will be here,
Waiting for you to return.
But my heart will go on.
One day, someone will
Sweep me off my feet.
You will lose me forever.
Please
don't let that happen.

MESSY ENDINGS AND CONFUSING CONVERSATIONS

Damn, I am going to miss you.
Dinner tonight — our first as ex-lovers.
I watch as you command the room
And all I can think is, "I will miss her."
You are so kind and tell great jokes.
Everyone loves and admires you.
You smile and laugh. I watch you dance.
All I can think is, "I, alone, truly know you."
I know your fears and insecurities.
I know your grit and I know your fight.
I miss our time and all that you are.
Please tell me how I can make this right.

FINN LYRIC

I never want to taste the bitter pill of settling.
There is a high from chasing the impossible.
I do not have to grasp it or hold on.
Just to touch it with my fingertip.
The chase, the journey, or the pursuit.
I fully acknowledge this breaks my own heart.
I fully acknowledge that this gives me life.

MESSY ENDINGS AND CONFUSING CONVERSATIONS

It ends the same way every time.
I go to your house and drive away crying.
Knowing that this is truly over.
Just say you hate me already.
So you don't want to talk.
Your kindness never ends.
Your kindness cuts deeper than a razor.
I cannot move on, when I still love you.

FINN LYRIC

I sat in that hospital parking lot for five days
As you watched your mother pass away.
I helped you pack up her old apartment.
I sat next to you as we mourned at the funeral.
I like it, when you call me your friend.
I love it, when I get to prove it.

Drowning in Sorrow

FINN LYRIC

I stumble when I step forward
Because I am looking back at you.
I can't turn around
Because you would turn away.
I used to think I would fight the world
To keep your love.
Now I am only fighting my own heart
To keep it in one piece.

MESSY ENDINGS AND CONFUSING CONVERSATIONS

While walking home I saw your car;
It was parked in front of my apartment.
You were coming back.
You were telling me you were wrong.
You were embracing me in your arms.
You were going to tell me you love me.
You were letting us be beautifully us.
I knew you would.
Twenty feet away I realized
It wasn't your car.

FINN LYRIC

The truth is...
I don't know anymore.
I can't trust my thoughts,
I can't trust my heart,
I can't trust my eyes.
I can trust that whatever choice I make
Will break my heart.

MESSY ENDINGS AND CONFUSING CONVERSATIONS

Being loved by you
Was like catching lightning in a bottle:
A once in a lifetime chance.
Now I have lost your love,
How can I hope to catch it again?
You cannot force it.
You cannot demand it.
You just wait...
And hope.

FINN LYRIC

Being *just friends* is killing me.
Do you know what it is like to cry on the way home?
The tears sting my eyes as I drive into a ditch.
The police officer does a sobriety test
Due to my red eyes.
As I tell him my story, he pities me.
The tow truck driver looks at me with disgust.
Now I am just crying at home.
Being *just friends* is killing me.

MESSY ENDINGS AND CONFUSING CONVERSATIONS

Yes, I cry.
Yes, I am in a dark spot.
Yes, I am lost.
Yes, I am confused.
Yes, I will survive.
Yes, I will grow stronger.
No, I am not giving up.

FINN LYRIC

You were the perfect moment.
You pulled me from the darkest place.
You invited me to a cabin in the woods.
You cheered for me as I ran.
You made your family mine.
You loved me for three years.
You brought peace to my chaos.
You were my favorite moment
But moments don't last.

MESSY ENDINGS AND CONFUSING CONVERSATIONS

Dear apartment ceiling,
I stare at you all the time.
What is it like watching me?
You watch me as I toss in bed.
You watch me endlessly write.
Are you disappointed when I text her back?
You've seen me cry.
You've seen me dissolve
Am I getting better?
Is my heart healing?
Am I getting over her?

FINN LYRIC

How do I tell my friends you are gone?
What do I say to your dad in the store?
How do I explain it to the people we know?
How do I ever look at the Grand Canyon
Without you next to me?
How do I hear our favorite songs
Without you singing along?
How do I walk into our restaurant alone
Without ordering your favorite dish?
How do I explain that
I wasn't enough?

MESSY ENDINGS AND CONFUSING CONVERSATIONS

If I was in a bar with you and a guy got too loud,
I would walk away with you.
If you wanted to see the world,
I would pack up the house and car.
I would walk away with you.
We planned on growing old.
If the good Lord called you home,
I would walk away with you.
I thought we had forever
But nothing good can last.
My dreams walked away with you.

FINN LYRIC

When I told you I had feelings for you,
You replied with, "I am not there yet."
When I told you I loved you,
You replied with, "I am not there yet."
When I said I would marry you,
You replied with, "I am not there yet."
I burned with passion, ready to jump in.
You, so cautious, loaded down with scars.
When you told me I had to move on,
I replied with, "I am not there yet."

MESSY ENDINGS AND CONFUSING CONVERSATIONS

I haven't told anyone you said goodbye.
If I did, it would feel like a betrayal of hope.
My friends and family keep asking about you.
I create the image from my delusion to smile.
I am embarrassed that I failed again,
That I drove into a ditch
Because I couldn't see the road through
My tears.
I choke up thinking of how I would explain
That I will never hold you again.
This empty apartment is full of sad songs
And shame.
My secret heartbreak

FINN LYRIC

Not texting you is killing me.
Your breadcrumbs haunt my mind.
I just want to talk to you
Like we used to.
But I don't want small talk.
I want to know how you are.
I want to hear how you sleep alone.
I want to see your eyes light up
When you talk about your friends.
I cannot like one more photo.
I need time to heal.
I need time to find myself. Just know...
Not texting you is killing me.

MESSY ENDINGS AND CONFUSING CONVERSATIONS

The feelings are gone.
I slip into apathy.
They were so strong
I couldn't carry them.
They carried me,
Directing me,
Guiding me.
Now the apathy has me.
Feel nothing.
Fake smiles.
Fake eye contact.
Fake interest.

FINN LYRIC

How are you?
In all my sadness,
I never asked.
Do you miss me?
Are you doing fine?
When work is hard
And the night is dark,
Do you miss me by your side?
Do you fake a smile?
Did you take down our pictures?
Did they leave marks in the wall,
A subtle reminder of what was?
Do you ever think of coming back?
When the wind howls
And the sleep won't come,
Do you talk to yourself?
Do you lie to yourself?
Do your tears salt your
Food as you eat alone?
With all that said:
How are you?

MESSY ENDINGS AND CONFUSING CONVERSATIONS

You asked me when I knew it was over.
I looked up with tears in my eyes.
I saw some clues but, deep down,
I don't know if I believe it is.

FINN LYRIC

Tomorrow I will see you again.
Whatever will I wear?
My heart on my sleeve.
I will be draped in mystery
With a patchwork of memories.
While dressed up with hope,
I will wear my scars like armor.
I will button up my emotions.
But all I want is the naked truth.

MESSY ENDINGS AND CONFUSING CONVERSATIONS

We were intertwined:
When they saw me,
They saw you.
This city is too small
To be without you.
Every corner
A memory of us,
A memory of love,
A memory of us.
Every building
Makes me miss you

FINN LYRIC

I went on a date tonight.
She was stunning,
The conversation was intriguing,
But she wasn't you.
It felt like a betrayal of what we were.
You will never know the ways
Your amazing love has ruined me.

MESSY ENDINGS AND CONFUSING CONVERSATIONS

I can't be your friend if we don't talk.
Tell me your secrets, tell me your thoughts,
Scream out your hopes, shout out your dreams,
Spill all your wishes, explain what they mean.
I can't be your friend if you bottle it inside.
Tell me of heartbreak and times that you lied.
Show me your scars and skeletons too.
We can figure it out and define what is true.
I will sit here and wait as long as it will take.
A friendship like ours will make the earth shake

FINN LYRIC

I got what I wanted:
A love that drove me crazy.
Now I am driving alone with
Tears running down my face.
A love that fills my head.
Now I can't stop thinking of
The way we said goodbye.
A love that is full of peace.
Now I sit alone in pieces.
I got what I wanted.

MESSY ENDINGS AND CONFUSING CONVERSATIONS

I am calling with no agenda.
I am calling with no plan.
Okay I admit that isn't true.
I absorb your every word.
I want to know if I can move on.
I want a reason to hate you.
Hating you would be easier.
Hating you could ease my mind.
Grasping at straws to hate or hope.
I cannot move forward.
I cannot move back.
I am paralyzed on the phone with you.

ANGER

45

FINN LYRIC

So what if I am broken? You are broken too.
I fought my doubts and fears.
You pushed away the one who loved you.
My brokenness drew me near.
Your brokenness left you alone.
My brokenness left you loved.
Your brokenness shook me to the bones

MESSY ENDINGS AND CONFUSING CONVERSATIONS

Medusa isn't a mythical monster.
She doesn't have snakes for hair.
Medusa is a 5-foot 7-inch woman
With beautiful blonde hair.
She is alive and well today.
Unlike me and my heart of stone.

FINN LYRIC

One day I will accept
That you are never
Coming back.
Not today,
But someday.

MESSY ENDINGS AND CONFUSING CONVERSATIONS

You breaking my heart
Was like leaving a house cat outside.
I didn't believe I could survive but
I became tough,
I became feral,
I became mean.
I am not the same;
I can never live inside again.

FINN LYRIC

With you I walked with confidence.
With you I loved myself in the mirror.
With you I slept in absolute peace.
With you I never felt out of place.
With you I never cried alone.
With you I loved myself.
I want to scream, "You stole that from me."
But how can you steal that which I never had?

MESSY ENDINGS AND CONFUSING CONVERSATIONS

Just like the night you said goodbye,
I cannot find the words.
The paper has nothing for me to write.
My mind is blank.
Panic fills me. Is it gone,
The words,
The feelings?
The drunkard is a coward.
Just like that night,
I have nothing to say,
Nothing to give.
Shame.

FINN LYRIC

Your mind is like a stream running through a forest.
My mind is like a ball of yarn rolling through combat.
Your mind guides you through choices like a gentle teacher.
My mind pushes and pulls me like a bodyguard trying to get me to safety.
Your mind can be a companion to share time with.
Mine terrifies me and I cannot be left alone with it.
Our minds are both beautiful, each serving in their own perfect way.
I won't change my mind

MESSY ENDINGS AND CONFUSING CONVERSATIONS

The man in the corner talking to himself.
The lady hitting the coin machine with angry fists.
The mother with a child harnessed to the folding table.
The grandmother guarding the wheeled basket.
The goon outside bumming cigarettes...
But I am the crazy one, thinking I can somehow wash the scent of you from my sheets. That I can wear these hoodies you bagged up on my porch, ones you won't wear again.
I am the crazy one, thinking that I can somehow just wash away the memory of you.

FINN LYRIC

I hate to look into your eyes.
The wreck of myself.
Shipwreck.
The eyes stare at me with disappointment.
I see that I am not enough.

MESSY ENDINGS AND CONFUSING CONVERSATIONS

I am finally over you
As long as I don't close my eyes.
I am finally over you
As long as I schedule every minute of my day.
I am finally over you
As long as I don't look online.
I am finally over you
As long as I don't see someone with blonde hair.
I am finally over you
As long as my phone never rings.
I am finally over you
As long as I don't look in the mirror.
I am finally over you
As long as the sun doesn't set or rise.

FINN LYRIC

I couldn't do it without you...
Then you proved me wrong.

MESSY ENDINGS AND CONFUSING CONVERSATIONS

I have to remember
You are making a choice.
Every day you don't call,
You are making a choice.
You don't want me anymore.
You are making a choice.
I choose peace.
I am making my choice

FINN LYRIC

Don't apologize to me;
Apologize to my future person.
I will never love that hard again.
She won't get 100% of me.
All the places we cannot go.
All the things we cannot do.
I always wondered where the broken come from.
They come from women like you.

MESSY ENDINGS AND CONFUSING CONVERSATIONS

I will figure it out.
I will learn how to eat alone.
I will learn how to sleep alone.
I will go to the beach by myself.
I will go into nature by myself.
Loneliness and solitude:
They are different beasts.
I will figure out solitude.

FINN LYRIC

Our love was born out of chaos;
It drew us together.
We learned to take on the world
Together.
Once we found peace,
You had no need for me.
Now I carry on
Fighting battles alone.

MESSY ENDINGS AND CONFUSING CONVERSATIONS

I would still burn down
This whole city for you
But now I would
Just stand in the flames.

FINN LYRIC

You could never break me.
I broke myself trying to love you.

MESSY ENDINGS AND CONFUSING CONVERSATIONS

I don't want to write any more sad poems.
I want to feel warmth reflect off my paper.
I want to revel about friendships and beauty.
But like spilled ink on paper, it is ruined by her

I won't pick up.
I won't let your words sting tonight.
You call me weak and petty.
I stand in good company.
The history of man is a story
Of the pettiness of weak men.

MESSY ENDINGS AND CONFUSING CONVERSATIONS

The slipping of the rope pulls the skin from my hand.
The hot pan burns my skin causing blisters to rise.
The desperate grasp of the blade cuts deep.
The rope, the pan, the blade.
My failures, my sorrow, my regrets.
I need to let go.
let go. Why can't I let go?

The Random Thought

67

FINN LYRIC

Watched my mom and dad pass
Without fear in their eyes.
I always thought they were so brave.
How can I have that peace when I die?
It is a long road that we travel down.
Life will teach and life will burn.
Know that loving will always bring pain
That makes you brave when it is your turn.

MESSY ENDINGS AND CONFUSING CONVERSATIONS

Mom and Dad, I miss you.
I made it. I am strong.
I find happiness in the sunrise.
I find joy in the little things.
I still go too hard on the weekends,
I still eat fast food,
But I make my bed.
I loved a woman and failed.
But I loved her right,
With no regrets.
I am a damn good dad.
Your granddaughter is like me;
She is as wild as the arctic wind.
I wish you could see me.
I wish we could talk one more time.
You would be proud.

FINN LYRIC

A fresh snowy walk in the city.
Early morning, the birds still asleep.
My steps are alone in the snow.
The streets are empty.
Shop lights guide my path
Like a crowd cheering me forward.
The hotels are full
But the lights are out.
Solitude in the city
Where there are no stars.
Quiet in the city
Where there is no rest.
Embrace this moment;
It will be gone in an hour

MESSY ENDINGS AND CONFUSING CONVERSATIONS

If you are happy,
Let it embrace you.
If you are scared,
Let it ignite you.
If you are sad,
Let it water your soul.
If you are angry,
Let it course through your veins,
Giving you purpose.

FINN LYRIC

Oh, hello Mr. Apathy.
I know you don't care
But I know you.
You act like you don't care.
The truth is you did.
One day you cared too much.
Your passion burned too hot.
You burned in the fire.
The hurt was too much.
Now you don't care,
That fire still burns.
Don't you dare extinguish it.

MESSY ENDINGS AND CONFUSING CONVERSATIONS

I have my mother's smile.
It only comes out when I feel real joy,
In moments in the sun,
Or with people I deeply love.
I will never have a pretty smile.
With the crow's feet edging my eyes,
The way my face contorts in bliss,
And the wrinkles on my forehead,
This is not a photo to show others.
It is not a photo to hang on the wall.
It is a photo I look at in my darkest times
And think, "I love to hate this photo."

FINN LYRIC

Friendship is a thing that doesn't make sense.
Friendship isn't logical and defies reason.
The friends that you bond with every day
Are rarely the ones who show up when
Your world crumbles and falls apart.
In your darkest moment a friend shows up:
They call you, they meet you, they carry you.
Then they slowly fade away
And leave an eternal mark.

MESSY ENDINGS AND CONFUSING CONVERSATIONS

Strange little creatures,
The human race.
We create so much pain
With a smile on our face.
We hurt each other
With the things we do.
We break hearts,
Say things that aren't true.
Even if you are perfect,
They'll lower you into the ground.
You just cause more pain
To all those gathered around.

FINN LYRIC

When I was a child
I just wanted fun friends.
When I was a teen
I just wanted cool friends.
When I was in my twenties
I just wanted successful friends.
When I was in my thirties
I just wanted a lot of friends.
Now that I am in my forties
I just want real friends.

MESSY ENDINGS AND CONFUSING CONVERSATIONS

Preparing to die
I know sounds dark.
I know it sounds sad.
I won't hurt myself
Or take my own life.
I don't want to be afraid,
Take the jump,
See scary places,
Touch the dangerous.
I want to leave nothing unsaid.
I want you to know I loved you.
You need to know my secrets
So I am writing my letters,
Finalizing my will,
Leaving nothing unsaid.

FINN LYRIC

Not everything I touch turns to gold;
Everything I touch turns to passion.
With passion comes hope and energy.
With passion comes hurt and pain.
The hope and energy carry me through the hurt and pain,
The long nights, the lonely days,
The heart-racing moments,
The crushing defeats and little victories.
There is a curse that is heavier than gold.

MESSY ENDINGS AND CONFUSING CONVERSATIONS

You are tougher than your toughest day.
Carrying your world is not the only way.
I know you're tired and the days are long.
You don your armor and carry on.
People develop their strength from watching you,
Not just in your strength but in your weakness too.
Strength in your sadness is the most beautiful of all.
With your people around you, you will never fall.

FINN LYRIC

I will never feel cold;
This heart burns too hot.
When the dark night comes,
I will walk straight through.
With all its scars and wounds,
It beats on with the thunder of hope.
The battles that come may seem too fierce
But this heart is ferocious and savage.
This untamed heart, rugged and tough,
Can only be held by the brave.
It is rowdy and unruly, wild at best,
But tested, loyal, and true

MESSY ENDINGS AND CONFUSING CONVERSATIONS

I miss war.
I miss the uncertainty of each day.
I miss the sweet life that is tasted each sunrise.
I long for the fellowship of warriors,
The faith in our commitment to each other.
I miss the excitement and laughter.
I miss the simplicity of just surviving.
The explosions and bullets don't scare me.
What the enemy couldn't do:
this boring life is
Killing me.

FINN LYRIC

I miss the feel of paper in my hand,
The smell of paper as I turn a page,
The way the corner folds as I rest,
The way the page is halfway turned
Before I finish the last sentence.
I miss the canvas's rough texture
As the brush glides over the clean surface,
The smell of each color as I free its potential,
The tubes of paint with their little creases
As the paint dries while I sit back and watch.
I need something real in this digital world.

MESSY ENDINGS AND CONFUSING CONVERSATIONS

The thoughts are like demons
Haunting my mind;
I exorcise them by putting them
On paper.

FINN LYRIC

I put on my uniform, Pick up my gun.
Do they know
I write poetry at night?
I look for perfect love.
I dream of a woman's embrace.
I put on my hard hat, Pick up my tools.
Do they know
I cry to songs on the radio?
I admire art alone.
I love romance.
In every man is a dichotomy:
I battle between soft and tough.
I stand as a mediator.
I refuse to allow either side to win.
To lose one is to lose myself.

MESSY ENDINGS AND CONFUSING CONVERSATIONS

I am glad you know exactly what you want.
Please know that you people are rare —
In the billions of people, there are few who do.
Be patient with us wanderers and explorers;
We go in a direction with a possible goal
But we get distracted by the flowers and sunsets.
We take detours and rarely stay on course.
We are wild and we are free.
We admire people like you: the solid and steady tree.

F#*! The Poetry Police
Your poem is too short.
Your poem is too long.
If it doesn't rhyme
Then it is wrong.
It doesn't describe in prolific words
The intricate placement of ideas,
Like the hands of time moving
Across the landscape of your body.
Your punctuation, is all wrong.
CaPiTaL letters don't belong there.
Line breaks have to be a certain way
Because it changes the flow.
Just keep writing.
Pour out your soul.
Put your thoughts on paper.
Just let it flow.
Try something new.
Try something wrong.
These are your poems.
These are your songs.

Healing

FINN LYRIC

I was broken and you didn't know.
I was lost in my own secret heartbreak.
You saw me from across the room
And your heart knew something was off.
That big smile caught my eye;
Every step closer, it grew larger.
You wrapped those big arms around me.
You squeezed all the pain out for a moment.
You took a deep breath in
And you held me for a few more seconds.
I wanted to crumble in your arms and weep.
You knew what nobody else did.
Your hug held me together for a moment

MESSY ENDINGS AND CONFUSING CONVERSATIONS

Bring on the hard days;
I can survive.
Bring on the tough times;
I can thrive.
This is what my life is made of:
Heartbreak, disappointment,
Loss, and grief.
I was born to suffer.
I am good at it.
That is why I cherish
Every moment of happiness.
That is why I am grateful
For a moment of peace.
That is why I love
Harder than anyone else.
My life has made me Grateful.

FINN LYRIC

I knew it wouldn't work out.
We were our own star-filled galaxies.
On our own, we existed beautifully.
Together we burned too hot.
Together we shone too bright.
While we collided, we were a sight to see.
Everyone watched in wonder.
Everyone gasped in awe.
We were one but now we are two.
Two star-filled galaxies growing apart —
Different, but just as beautiful as ever.

MESSY ENDINGS AND CONFUSING CONVERSATIONS

Waiting for you is easy.
I can control how much you hurt me.
Waiting for you is easy.
I can remember the times we were happy.
Waiting for you is easy.
I can hope that you will see your mistake.
Waiting for you is easy.
I don't have to heal or move on.
Waiting for you is easy.
I don't have to tell our friends.
Waiting for you is easy.
I can pretend it is a season.
Waiting for you is easy.
I am not alone, with you in my memory.
Waiting for you is easy.
I only have a half-broken heart.
Waiting for you is easy.
I just keep believing my lies.
You're not coming back.
There won't be a phone call.
You're not coming back.
I will have to heal.
You're not coming back.

FINN LYRIC

I feel a strange comfort in your apathy.
When I see you and you don't care,
It is the closest thing I will ever find to closure.
I can't rely on you to give me what I need.
I will leave it to you to bottle things up.
I will wear my heart on my sleeve for me
And only me.

MESSY ENDINGS AND CONFUSING CONVERSATIONS

I run to my sisters:
The heartbreak fixers.
One won't show up but will text.
One will comfort me.
One will sit in silence with me.
One will take me to a dirty bar.
One will throw me a party.
So my sisters will be there,
Heal my heart and love me

FINN LYRIC

I need to put down the drink,
Stop going out to hide from it,
Pull down my strongman mask,
Take a moment to stare into the pit.
I know that this is going to hurt,
To take in the pain and loss,
Face the fact I have to be alone.
The road to healing always has a cost.

MESSY ENDINGS AND CONFUSING CONVERSATIONS

The sun is out today.
I am capturing my thought.
I am finding the peace,
Quitting the battles I fought.
It may be exhaustion;
The fire just won't burn.
As I watch the birds fly free
I think maybe it is my turn,
My turn to see a better day,
A chance to make myself right,
Take it all in and breathe.
I can just bask in the light.
I know the dark will come.
I will make it through the night.
For the first time in a long time
I finally have my sight.

FINN LYRIC

You sat at the table behind me.
I could hear your laughter.
You looked amazing in your dress.
It should have been me next to you.
I played my part. I knew my role.
My tuxedo covered my fears.
You happy is all I wanted to see.
Now it is back to picking up the
Pieces of me.

MESSY ENDINGS AND CONFUSING CONVERSATIONS

I woke up this morning.
For the first time,
I felt the warmth of the sun
And smiled at the man in the mirror.
For a moment I knew
Everything would be okay.
It was only a moment
But it was true

FINN LYRIC

As the warm water flows over me
I rinse away the cruel day.
I try to forget all the cruel things I say.
The feel of soap feels slick on my skin.
I wash away the dirt on my skin.
I try to forget the man I have been.
As I shave my head, the scraping of skin.
My hair falls out as I grow old.
I remember that my story's untold.

MESSY ENDINGS AND CONFUSING CONVERSATIONS

Gratitude isn't like hope.
You have to mine gratitude.
You have to dig deep.
You have to experience
Hardship,
Heartbreak,
Pain,
Defeat.
Each difficulty is a morsel,
A tiny piece put in a vault,
A vault of the soul.
The riches of gratitude
Make the sweetness sweeter,
Hardships easier,
And love greater.

FINN LYRIC

When friends become lovers:
What a dangerous game.
No favorite color.
No learning new names.
They will feel like home,
Easy to talk to and easy to call.
When you love a friend,
You risk it all.
When a friend breaks your heart,
When a friend walks away,
That's a real deep pain,
One that never goes away.

MESSY ENDINGS AND CONFUSING CONVERSATIONS

Let it be.
Rest.
Sleep in.
Breathe.
Wrap yourself in comfort.
Allow yourself to be.
It will be alright.
You will be alright.

FINN LYRIC

Getting over you is a hell of a climb:
The cliffs are steep,
Crumbling with every grasp.
Fingers bleed from my death grip.
The ropes are showing wear.
My legs tremble in weakness.
Your last words blow in the wind.
The coldness stings my face.
This journey is one I never wanted.
I know the view from the top
Will be beautiful
But surviving the climb is all I can do.

MESSY ENDINGS AND CONFUSING CONVERSATIONS

I will love again.
My soul will carry on.
Time will slowly tick on as I grow old.
My heart is too big to be alone.
This time I will wait to find the right one.
They will sweep me off my feet.
With their eyes, they will grasp my soul.
We will talk for hours about our day.
We will travel to places we have never seen.
I just really hope it's you.

FINN LYRIC

The doctor gave me the pills,
Promised to take off the edge.
But I want to feel all the pain.
I want to trust the process.
I hate the way I feel right now.
It will fertilize my soul.
Not where I want to be
But where I need to be

MESSY ENDINGS AND CONFUSING CONVERSATIONS

To strong love, messy endings, and confusing conversations,
The sour lemon, the bitter herb, and spicy flavors of life.
There is no room for boredom or apathy in a lover's heart.
It will be wonderful, terrifying, and exciting in a moment.
A lover's life is ugly and beautiful at the moment of that first broken
heart.
Carry on, lover. Learn, lover.
Love harder, love softer, love better.
Love yourself, lover. Love yourself.

Goodbye

FINN LYRIC

108

MESSY ENDINGS AND CONFUSING CONVERSATIONS

One day I will accept
That you are never
Coming back.
Not today,
But someday.

FINN LYRIC

It is time for me to stop,
Stop loving her.
It is time for me to grow,
Grow by myself.
It is time to move on,
Move to peace.
It is time to stop wasting time
On people I love.
It is time to love
The people who love me.

MESSY ENDINGS AND CONFUSING CONVERSATIONS

Do you want to see a trick?
I do it with my eyes.
Look deeply into them.
They are blue.
That isn't it.
Here it is.
Watch closely.
They only ever
Saw the good in you.
They reflected
The love you gave me.
They saw our
Entire future in a moment.
Oh, you can't see the trick?
Well, I have been crying a lot
Lately.

FINN LYRIC

Some people thrive in chaos.
Others thrive in silence.
Some thrive in the daily routine.
I thrive in pain.
A moment to rebuild on rubble.
A moment to realize what is important.
A moment to throw away the insignificant.
I thrive in simple survival

MESSY ENDINGS AND CONFUSING CONVERSATIONS

I fall for it every time:
Your glances,
Your small talk.
I don't know if we can be friends.
I can't minimize our past
To pretend for the future.
You are not just a person;
You were my person.

FINN LYRIC

Let me be and watch. Let me go feral.
Let me run amok in the human dynamic.
I put on masks and try on attitudes with every new encounter.
Watch me socially frolic like a child in costume.
I dance through conversations with ease,
Pulling others into my social masquerade ball.
This is who I am meant to be for the next five minutes.

MESSY ENDINGS AND CONFUSING CONVERSATIONS

Can I ask you a question?
One final question.
Are you happier now?
Are you at peace
Now that you walked away?
All I ever wanted:
You to be happy,
You to be at peace.
Now I can have happiness.
Now I can have peace.

FINN LYRIC

I gave you the role in the play
That you never wanted.
The script in my head was perfect
And you played your part beautifully.
But you, the actress, changed the story.
You stole the show.
Now I am behind the curtain,
Watching you shine.

MESSY ENDINGS AND CONFUSING CONVERSATIONS

I have to run.
I will leave you with this:
I need a new scene.
A year in Europe
Will cleanse my soul.
This city is too small
To move on from you.
I thought I was strong
But I am admitting I am weak.
Give me a year.
I will see you back here
With a sense of real peace,
With a smile on my face.

FINN LYRIC

Dear Reader,

I tried to endure this pain, to push through, but I've reached my limit. The heartbreak I've been carrying has overwhelmed me, more than I ever thought it could. Losing her wasn't just losing a person—it felt like losing a part of myself, a part I thought would always be there. She wasn't just someone I loved; she was my best friend, my confidant, my safe space. And now, the connection we once shared has been reduced to occasional, impersonal messages about logistics, devoid of the warmth and understanding that once defined us.

I promised her I'd remain a friend, that I'd stay in her life in some way, but I'm realizing now how much I underestimated the weight of that promise. It's harder than I could have ever imagined—to be close but distant, to care so deeply yet have to hold back. Every interaction is a reminder of what we've lost, and the ache of that reality feels like it's pulling me apart.

Next month, I'll be starting a new chapter with a position in Europe. While the idea of fresh beginnings is appealing, the truth is, I'm running away—not toward new opportunities, but from the grief, the memories, and everything that reminds me of her. Staying here feels unbearable, so I'm choosing distance, hoping it will ease the pain. Yet, even as I prepare to leave, a part of me feels ashamed, knowing that running won't erase the hurt; it will just change the scenery.

Still, I'm holding on to hope. Writing has been my anchor in all of this, and I know it will continue to be as I navigate the healing process. I've already started working on my next poetry book—a collection inspired by everything I'm feeling and learning during this time. I hope, when the time comes, you'll look forward to reading it.

For now, all I can do is keep moving forward, one day at a time... one word at a time.

Sincerely,

Finn Lyric

About the Author

Finn Lyric is a poet whose work captures the raw beauty of love and heartbreak, channeling the resilience and grit of a life lived on the edge. Born and raised in the rugged landscapes of Alaska, Finn's poetry reflects the stark contrasts of his home—wild, untamed, yet profoundly tender.

A former Army Ranger, Finn's experiences in the military shaped his deep appreciation for human connection and the fragility of life. Now working in construction, he finds inspiration in the rhythm of hard labor and the quiet solitude of rebuilding.

Finn's verses are both reflective and cathartic, a mosaic of passion, loss, and healing that resonates with readers searching for authenticity and depth. Writing under his pseudonym, Finn Lyric, he offers a window into the universal struggle of holding onto love in an unpredictable world.